C000178728

FUR

First published in 2015 by
The Dedalus Press
13 Moyclare Road
Baldoyle
Dublin 13
Ireland

www.dedaluspress.com

Copyright © Grace Wells, 2015

ISBN 978 1 910251 12 6

All rights reserved.
No part of this publication may be reproduced in any form or by
any means without the prior permission of the publisher.

The moral right of the author has been asserted.

Dedalus Press titles are represented in the UK by
Central Books, 99 Wallis Road, London E9 5LN
and in North America by Syracuse University Press, Inc.,
621 Skytop Road, Suite 110, Syracuse, New York 13244.

Cover image: The Fawn, © duncan1890 / iStockPhoto

The Dedalus Press receives financial assistance from
The Arts Council / An Chomhairle Ealaíon

FUR

Grace Wells

DEDALUS PRESS
DUBLIN, IRELAND

for Lani O'Hanlon

Then draw near to nature. Then try, like some first human being, to say what you see and experience and love and lose.

— Rainer Maria Rilke

ACKNOWLEDGEMENTS

Acknowledgements and thanks are due to the editors of the following magazines and periodicals in which some of these poems, or versions of them, first appeared:

Dublin Poetry Review, Poetry Ireland Review, Prairie Schooner, The Shop, The Stinging Fly, Toe Good Poetry, The Poetry Bus, Waterford Healing Arts Trust Poetry Menu.

And to RTE's *Sunday Miscellany* program.

Poems have also been included in the following anthologies:

Shine On: Irish Writers for Shine, edited by Pat Boran, Dedalus Press (2011); *What We Found There,* edited by Theo Dorgan, Dedalus Press (2013); *Windows 20 Years,* edited by Heather Brett and Noel Monahan, Windows Publications; *Where Beach Meets Ocean,* edited by Lisa Starr, Block Island Poetry Project (2013)

The author would like to extend her sincere gratitude to the Arts Council of Ireland, and to South Tipperary County Council for bursary support, and also to Kilkenny County Council and Waterford City & County Council who have continued to offer employment opportunities that have helped keep the wolf from the door. Thanks are also due to the Heinrich Böll Cottage and to Château de Lavigny, whose residencies were fundamental to the development of this manuscript.

For their wisdom and warm friendship, very special thanks must go to poets Pat Boran, Mark Roper, Paddy Doyle, James Harpur, Mary O'Gorman, Thomas McCarthy and Lani O'Hanlon.

Contents

BECOMING ANIMAL

CORNUCOPIA

⤳

The Cultured World

Achill

It started on Achill, October
and autumn light on the fern hills, mountains
crowned in Paul Henry cloud.

I cycled beneath them energised,
girlish as the heroine
of a nineteen-fifties film.

At Dugort dolphins put on a private show,
inland a kestrel allowed me
follow her hunt through the marsh fields.

To the house a robin came each day
tapping the window,
insistent as a messenger.

There was something wrong
about my nightly phone-calls home
as if the island were just too far off

and I could no longer quite be reached.
I kept company with gulls
and oystercatchers, birds

braving the wild currents of air.
On Achill it is all about flight,
anything insufficiently tethered breaks loose.

I could not read the portents,
it is only now I know the unravelling
began there—the salt breath

off the Atlantic and the lungs
unable to harbour such freedom.
I must warn you not to go there

unless you are able for that sea wind,
unless you are ready to change your life.

Vixen

i.
Christmas night you conjured her—
turkey leavings left in a bowl by the door.

Then mornings of bones strewn like the *I Ching*.
Whatever you left was taken.

Out of winter's blue-black ink she came.
Always at night. Withheld.

It was weeks before we saw her,
a sleekness hugging shadow,

wildness, taken on form, to step into our yard.

ii.
She became our shy presence.
We'd drive home to startle her in headlights.

We raided the fridge for her, invented scraps,
only for her to retreat

and return. She brought us
the part of our selves that wasn't fully human.

Sometimes, beyond reach of the yard lamp,
she curled by the gate, waiting.

And I longed to go with her.

iii.
Spring screams set our nights on fire,
we woke to yearning tearing our paper walls,

siren cries, something like torture;
night glutted with her sounds,

we hugged each other for comfort,
awed by howl and answer—

by whatever it is that longing does
when it meets itself in the woods.

Islanded on the territory of her rut,
we were solidities her cries resounded off—

she took us into her mating,
included us, as surely other nights

we had included her.

iv.
Then silence. You abroad, so I was alone
when out from her dark gestation, she came.

She spurned me: a mistrustful slink,
back and forth over the field.

Only following her tracks, I saw them.
One after another, a litter of cubs.

v.
The young grew bold; age or curiosity
getting the better of them,

and they followed her—little ink-tipped marvels—
out of meadow grass, onto our lawn.

I tried to keep quiet, to protect them,
but there was nothing secret about their circus;

they drew the crowd, friends flocked
eager for the pleasure and wonder.

Our summer commune. Columbine, then roses,
and foxes like a blessing. We were rich with them

until the unmarked day, when the wild caught up with us—
and without warning, they disappeared.

Selkie Moment

She rose from the warmth of their bed,
in the kitchen cut her hair,

the loss of it could not sever love
for holding him she'd held the cultured world—

only she had found where he kept her pelt
beneath the dry earth of their barn.

Shrunken, matted, its pulse gone—
but a claw still scratched

and the scratch called for salt and change.
She put the skin onto her back

walked out into darkness. Seal-headed,
swam beneath the myriad brilliant stars.

Queue

They are at the back of an impossible queue
inching forward, dragging luggage,
pretending not to eye their fellow passengers.

He has his arm around her, and every so often
he pulls her to his body as if they were back
in their airport hotel moving over one another.

Only the airless shuffle toward the man
who'll take their passports and ask his questions.
They have been in the queue forever,

they will remain in it forever, there is no sense
of time moving forward, they cannot see the queue
will end, that within a year they'll be back

staying overnight in that same hotel, that again
they'll roll over each other, lost in the world
of their private sonar, nor that in the morning

she will deliver him to the terminal, embrace him
one final time, before stepping back into her car
and driving away—from him,

from everything that for so long she has called love.

Animal Encounters

What They Have Done with Kilkenny

See, there was a cormorant on the weir,
still as a prayer in the centre of the city,
its black wings spread like a heraldic crest
and I stopped Dave to make him look,

the river glass smooth, a blue mirror
to the sky, evening light and a bride
posing on a hotel balcony, the white ripples
of her dress running to meet and merge

with the black, spread feathers of that bird.
It was all archetype. I had not long since
clinked my glass to Dave's, laughed *To us,*
only to fumble apology. I hadn't meant

to suggest anything, but we were drinking
in the cavern of a tapas bar
and, while I blushed, the high heels
of hen parties clicked the curbs

in skirts so short they were hardly skirts.
Stags reared their heads, shifted from one
watering hole to the next, baying a rut
between the bunny girls, the hula girls

and the tinsel pink women in cowboy hats.
The day had been full of such things.
I had only just said goodbye
to a different man, a married man,

and when we hugged to part,
our bodies burst into flame, the spoors
of him on me all weekend, especially then,
in that bar and later when I led Dave

down to the river, where the bride
on the happiest day of her life grinned
into the evening light and the cormorant
lifted its wings above the weir,

like it was me spreading the dark arms
of my wildness and, risen nude, dripping
river mud, had stepped from water
into a city where anything could happen next.

Summer

and the usual chaos of children
and home-maintenance.

Summer and I am slowly
turning into my house.

And stealing
one small slip of time

I hurry to the studio
at the bottom of my garden,

harried there, spat out
like an owl pellet,

every good part of me
consumed.

All I intend is
to write it down,

to add one more sentence
to the pile

of how it feels to have language
drilled from the tongue.

But waiting for me, on the path,
on its every flagstone, are butterflies,

peacock butterflies,
purple, scarlet, bronze.

Return of the Salmon

after Ted Hughes's 'Night Arrival of Sea Trout'

All night I waited.

Early mist and rowan berries scarlet
in the waking stream announced

their coming like a telegraph.
In dawn light the earth sang beneath her breath.

Hazel-nuts tumbled from her skirts
and the larks ran on ahead,

carrying her tune above the moor
and downstream

to the stubble fields and the Horned God
running, leaping with his drum.

Autumn

It is autumn again
and I'm not ready.

Handy then
that you should give me

this scrap of hessian, the *rough,
dumb country stuff* that I adhere to.

Whoever stitched it
sews as I do,

with an uneven hand,
with the understanding

that even torn things
may be patched together.

I need this flint arrowhead
for there's flesh to be cut from old wounds,

and now the cold
has come again

I'll take this button
for my coat—

its pockets may be empty
but into the lining

I have sewn
a minute envelope.

It holds the twenty-six letters
of the alphabet

and one full-stop.
Potent as a bullet

or a kiss.

Folktale

i.
Ten years we lived beside each other
and nothing between us, nothing more
than politeness, the courtesies

that exist between a woman
and the husband of her best-friend.
Then you drew your hand along my skin.

No, I said.
No, I said.
No, I said again.

But still you followed after,
walking through the night to my door.
I had already quenched the lamp

but you were reaching out
of long years, slitting
the wolf's belly for survival.

I sewed the pelt closed.
For months we met there.
Mute, we lived by the language of the body;

such words may not be written down—
have no translation. Wolf-bloodied,
fur-touched, we were changed and carnal.

Early spring, growth in the fields,
I caught a scent of earth stirring,
something tender happening elsewhere.

ii.
Witch, you led
through the woods
to the white bed
where he lay as an offering.

Indian-giver, your mouth
was full of lies.
When I fell
there was no stopping it.

From then on, if we met,
there was a corpse between us
and nothing to protect you
from the axe of my hand.

iii.
It wasn't strange to me when two Alsatians
took down the sheep you grazed in my field.

You left her carcass there to rot. I was the one
to gather in the soft, wasted pelt of her fleece.

Long afterward, you were both still barking
your denials, so I never could explain

our story, nor your need
to lead me blindfold

down the corridor of trust
and put my hands to the door marked *Bereft*.

Our Myth was a Garden of Eden

each of us moving in turn
through Adam and Eve,

and the serpent entwining
my trees until I acquiesced

as women are wont to do
from pressure or compassion.

But the sweet taste
was nothing to the aftershock.

For a year I was Eve's sorrowing
and the fire in me was Adam's rage

and in the garden I was snake
shedding a necessary skin.

Like Persephone Emerging from the Underworld

Scent of damp and lightless earth, and rain dripping a music
that guides her through the woven cage of a yew.

Fruit trees pruned of limbs, and at her feet
the rusted bolt of a leaf that will not open.

Bark on a eucalyptus strung up and lamenting.
Hydrangea, a fist of sticks pointing blame.

Mint pushed so far into the ground it cannot rise.
Sorrel leapt to seed as though it can no longer trust.

Then a blur of black wings like a dark thought—
and she knows she has been rich in dark thought too long.

Raindrops on rose thorns glimmer, cherry petals
fall like tickertape, daffodils announce an armistice.

Pink camellia lie fallen and bruised, but buds on
that same camellia insist she find courage to live again,

to risk future descents,
however they come, however many.

A still pond and in it reflected sky.
She can barely look such blue in the face.

An insect lands on her lapel—a winged creature of white air.

Otter

Some things happened that should not have,
I made mistakes and was given witness to my worst self—

I was left like something a spider leaves,
sucked of everything except despair.

We founder and must find ways to mend.
One foot in front of the other I walked the riverbank,

inland, upstream, letting water flow against my failings.
I struck a path through cow-parsley and nettle,

holding the indigo lamp of bluebells to my damage,
moving deeper toward the river's quiet country,

further into my personal ruin. Where the two
converged I slumped among the wet weeds, wanting

the river to wash right through me, to wipe me clean.
And up from the liquid surface rose an otter;

an otter plunging the water. It dived to somersault,
to divide in two and become a mated pair.

Black as eels but halo-bright they circled, swimming
me into their carnival, into a wider world—

so that I want to say, do not fear your anguish;
despair births miracles; hope is only waiting for release.

Pay attention, the signs gifted are subtle: small beads
for the necklace of faith we must thread for ourselves.

Animal Encounters

It was a small kitchen and hot,
no proper work surfaces, no ventilation—
but the ants didn't mind. Evenings they came

unspooling through the pantry, unwinding
over cupboards, probing for any crumb.
And one night I came home late, drunk,

to find the place infested, a black flood
of ant armies travelling like neurons
straight to my instincts, direct to murderous rage.

I went at them as if they
had declared war on my children.
I don't want to tell you the things I did.

All week I had been thinking
about animal encounters—
the messages creatures bring.

For so long I had wanted
to read augury,
to grow fluent in omen.

So what could it portend, a woman
in her midnight kitchen—
a crazed exterminator

bashing at ants with her broom,
pouring boiling water,
scooping her dark harvest into a pail?

Canvas

In the afternoon I walked the beach hounded by longing.
The sky was white and pink and blue, somewhere it was

silver for the surface of the sea had that same iridescence.
Sea and sky were one—a canvas the light passed over.

All year I had been metallic, creased as tin-foil, stiff
with anger; my only softness a wound I could not heal.

Betrayal does this—though if I told you the story, you would
want time to think it over, to ask who betrayed whom?

I walked the sand beneath a flock of oystercatchers, their wings
black and white arrows pointing direction,

urging me back to the human world but when I looked
there was only a woman walking her dogs

and my greeting frightened her as if my need for touch
was a knife that could attack, so I called

to the shells and stones, to driftwood along the shore,
asking where should I put my body so it might be answered.

But the waves didn't care, the shells didn't speak,
the gulls only laughed. I was a walking part of everything,

the sky moved overhead. I turned charcoal, white, ultramarine.

Each Day the Queen Wasp Came

at first I thought it always the same creature—
September turning to October and her regular flight
in through any open window—but then two came. Three.

October yielded to November and still they came
buzzing their insistent daily drone, demanding
their abundance was a portent I should read.

Lone sovereigns, I feared everything about them:
their sickening clash of black and yellow armour,
all that latent, formidable power, as though

when they flew into my rooms, I'd drawn a dark card,
Death or The Tower reversed and they heralded
transformation through some unavoidable sting.

Late autumn, last leaves on the chestnut,
I faced my fears, researched wasps, tracing
my fortune between the lines of science. *Come*

they whispered, *it is time to over-winter. Be tenacious.*
Live by the lamp of your own scent, Queen wasp, complete.
Not ready for any voice to tell me I was built

for such aloneness, I almost gave up divination—
but then I read how few queens survive,
that if they live, they only live a year

and I knew the wasps didn't care
about my aloneness or whatever I might
or might not achieve, they were saying,

Do this for me: love with abandon the physical world.

Gold Scarab, Rose Chafer

for Lyn and Mathew Mather

i.
Their sessions repeat themselves. She leads
him through a narrow maze, passing
familiar exhibits, returning to habitual walls.

Then she dreams. Night gifts her a golden scarab.
As she describes the beetle to him, a tap
at the window pulls his hand to the latch

and what flies to his palm is a rose-chafer—
a European scarab. When the gift is presented
to her a second time, the rose-chafer flies free,
                          and the healing commences.

ii.
I love this story—it is never done with me.
Like the insect in Jung's hand, I am
perpetually held in the story's curl.

At heart it is a story about a dream
and a dream can change everything—
sleep reels-in symbols that we fly toward,

the way my girlish hand once flew
to emerald scarabs in a Bangkok market.
It was long before I had heard Jung's story

but even then I was reaching for my self—
the way we all reach for our essence
only to leave that shimmering aspect

outside, beyond glass, while some foolishness
in us turns away and draws down the shades.
I have come to think we must be alert,

always open, ever ready to receive
the smallest agent of transformation,
for that is what the story is,

and I never tire of its telling;
nor the way I'm lit each time
the rose-chafer is released into a room,

whispering again that the language
of this world is amelioration.

Being Human

Ten Chairs

There is little light-hearted
about these chairs. No!
These are serious chairs.
All ten of them. All different.
Chairs of oak and ash and pine.
One is a súgán chair
and one made entirely of coiled straw.
These chairs came from a house
famous for music,
and a house famous for stories,
and a house that no longer stands.

These chairs are dense with the lean times,
the hard times, the times
of want and danger.
They were scraped over flag-floors
that wept in certain weathers,
they were saved for Sundays,
they were the only chairs.
There must once have been
thousands of such chairs;
they must have gone
from circulation one by one.

Now in this room these chairs
are oral history.
Pass round the clay pipes,
let there be talk of rain
and how the dog fox has been
barking in the early dawn.
These chairs are the congregation

of a townland,
they know about laughter
and easy mirth. Later
they will be pushed back
for the dancing—

but remember there is little
light-hearted here,
only some playful aspect
in their arrangement—
row upon row—
recalls a childhood game
where everyone must run
in a circle and dive for a seat
when the music stops,
except there are never enough
chairs to go round.

It is after all a serious game
meant to teach us how fragile we are,
how precarious the fates,
how easy to be out of the running.

The Long Corridor

after Dennis O'Driscoll

We came too late,
the long corridor of the seminary
emptied of its years
of footfall and trespass.

The wax flowers remained
and biblical scenes in sombre oils.
There were certain large pieces
of immovable furniture

and polish over everything.

But no votive offerings,
no one kneeled before candles
or asked forgiveness,
or rose against the dark.

There were rooms off the corridor
that we could not go into,
built of impervious granite,
with bars on the windows—

and though it defied belief,
we saw for ourselves
they had bricked up
children in the walls.

Bosnia 2015

A bag can be made from a woman's skin.
Into mine I put mountains and white snow.
Into mine I put flowers for his grave.

In the camp they made a cookbook, a father's
dumplings, a mother's bread, an aunt's favourite cake.
In the camp they shared the imagined feast.

I would like to have seen my son's page,
to know what he was thinking of, purple borscht,
caraway seed, the chopping of an onion.

The men who took him live two streets away.
My wish is for a local court, for all of us
to stand on grass and speak our truth.

But their facts are not mine
and in the absence of shared history
there is less and less to say.

The Pain Index of Writer's Block

after the Schmidt Sting Pain Index

*"I've always been blocked as a writer but my desire
to write has been so strong that it has always broken
down the block and gone past it."*
— *Tennessee Williams*

0.2   Mild irritation, like losing a thought
on the tip of your tongue.

1.0   Perpetual frown, as if straining liquid
through a sieve partially clogged
with pips and seeds.

2.5   An unexpected sense of loss and injustice
comparable to standing naked by the bath
and finding there's no hot water.

3.8   Nagging exasperation, similar to being
stuck in rush-hour traffic
on a wet Friday in December.

4.6   Growing malcontent, like having a mouse
living in the walls of your bedroom
and being unable to trap it.

5.0   Frustrating sense of isolation akin
to the second day of a cold, head
congested, eyes streaming.

5.5   Turgid constriction, picture a gutter
choked with decayed and foul-smelling leaves.

6.0	An on-going, season-long suppression of spirit.
7.2	A slow-burning injustice in the bones like being sent to the Gulag for a crime you did not commit.
8.5	Life-threatening, tempestuous pain. Imagine a dolphin thrashing in a net off Taiji, Japan.
9.0	The wind-pipe has closed. You live without air.
10.0	Elements of all of the above, combining to numb the body: the paralysis of observing years pass and not sitting down to that first precious word.

Poem for Tennessee Williams

"None of my essential personality problems are solved.
I have not found the sustained desirable lover.
No new convictions—no new lamp-post
on the dark road I am stumbling crazily along.
I think I grow steadily a little bit harder and emotionally tougher—
not what I want."
—Tennessee Williams, New Orleans, October 29th 1941

All year you've stung with the failure
of your first play—the critics' howl
that it was *Amateurish, Repugnant*;
the Censor called in
to investigate its *putrid* lines.

Your mother echoes disappointment,
she finds your work *ugly, indecent*
and *a disgrace to her kinfolk.*
Wary of offending her Southern manners,
your letters home omit the truth of your days.

I don't believe anyone ever suspects
how completely unsure I am
of my work and myself.

On the other side of the world, war.
The theatres demand patriotic entertainment.
From a friend you borrow a typewriter
and put it in hock for a meal ticket.
Your weak eye needs a cataract operation,

an impacted tooth must be pulled, but not yet:
for now you must cultivate friends
who give dinners, live on fifty dollars

a month, accept *the squalor, the awkwardness
and indignity* of being broke.

*What we need is writing
that gets at the fundamental falsehoods
and stupidities that make the world
such a nightmare for most of its people.*

Through practise you have become
horribly expert in the administration
of palliative drugs—
amusements, indulgences,
little temporary evasions and escapes.

On Royal Street you room opposite
the St James, from the balcony you
*hover like a bright angel over the troubled
waters of homosociety.* Only true friends
know how you spend your nights.

*I am moving. A misunderstanding
about some sailors who come in occasionally
to discuss literature with me
provoked a tedious little quarrel
with the land-lady—I told her
I could not live in such an atmosphere
of unwarranted suspicion.*

December. The Japanese have bombed
Pearl Harbour. You are borrowing
against your gabardine suit. You wish
for a simple life *with epic fornications*
and make a religion of endurance.

Shore patrols and MPs raid the gay bars,
the life is going out of New Orleans.
But tonight there's a party
in the Vieux Carré.
While you are out

I aim to slip into your low lit room.
I plan to leave some bank notes
on your dresser. I want to thank you
for lines you are yet to write.
I want to tide you over.

At the Festival

we danced under a harvest moon,
there was drumming, and firelight,
and children wore flowers in their hair.

We walked naked through the fields,
washed in communal showers,
dug our toilets in the wood.

At the festival there were initiation rites—
the boys went out into the wilderness
and came back as men.

The days began with songs for universal peace—
fathers sobbed openly
and women keened for their dead.

All week we watched sun and shadow
pass over the purple mountains,
there was never rain without a rainbow.

But at the festival people kept forgetting
to put their milk in the shade,
it soured and went solid in the carton.

I don't know how many times I emptied
sour milk into the ditch. It was on
my sixth or seventh journey

that I lost it, found myself weeping among
the hazels and hawthorn,
not understanding my grief.

It took Conflict-Resolution Tomas
accusing me of stealing his carton
before it all made sense:

I was crying
for my mother who never
could waste anything,

*crying for the luxury of camping
in a field beside you, Tomas,*

*when my father and both my grandfathers
had to give up everything to kill your people.*

Ekphrasis

for my mother

Here then is your war, a daylight raid over London,
the sky a formation of silver planes and beneath them
a girl in a slipper fragile as glass. And if a hero
could return its pair, you would dance again
with your Daddy in a house overlooking the park.

There are blue drapes in the painting, you keep one hand
to their velvet, one foot anchored to the golden rug.
Like a tightrope walker you set your chin firm.
For years I held your failings against you,
but all along you were only practicing your art.

The Naming

All this happened in a previous century,
frost whitened the tops of trees, water froze.

By day a curl of smoke unfurled
from the cottage chimney into still air.

On a full moon night she came.

As was the custom
they kept the child un-bathed for three days,

then fetched water from the mountain stream
and washed her in a basin by the fire.

The father had taken oaken boards
to make a cradle.

The babe fed at her mother's breast.
It was the trees that held her name.

Boughs singing with the wind
they placed their breath in her.

Waxen leaves, needle-pointed for strength
they placed their mind in her.

Hope-bright, scarlet berries
they placed their heart in her,

Holly, Holly, Holly.

The Forgetting

for Holly

Forgive me child but this is The Forgetting
and while you sleep

I must disarm you of Kali,
I must rob you of her strength.

Forgive me as I pull the rhythm of hooves from your bones,
as I extract the wildness of Epona neighing.

Forgive me as I take Venus from your body,
as I erase Parvati and Aphrodite, Goddesses of love.

From our house I have cleared
all signs of Hestia, keeper of the hearth,

for this is The Forgetting and you must cease to think
of Freya and Fortuna, of Fauna who guards the woods.

In the face of injustice do not call on Maat and Themis,
do not send your hot anger to Skadi, Goddess of Winter.

Forget her. Forget Athena, forget Artemis,
forget Atoja who sends the rains.

Do not think again of Asherah
who brought our earth into being

and let it go unsaid that the ground
beneath your feet is the living Gaia.

When you wake from this your tongue
will no longer remember the old prayers,

forgive me, but in this place you must do as they instruct,
put your hand to your breast, here, here,

repeat after me, father, son,
Holy Ghost.

Pyx

for Holly Wells, born October 1991, murdered in Soham,
England, August 2002;
and for my daughter, Holly Wells, born November 1994

Plaster, gilding, pigment, stitches on unbleached canvas,
I will put these things into a poem,

grief-struck, dumb-mouthed,
knowing there has been a journey

into the chaos of myth
and no safe return from Dis.

How to measure the weight
of what each of us carries beneath the skin?

Where to turn for a cure?
Must it be this persistent stare at tragedy,

the wish for revelation,
for a clarity we could wear on the wrist like a watch—

or, like a locket, which could open repeatedly
to show love made visible.

For you I make this pyx a tabernacle,
let the livid bruise do its work,

let this inhuman purple
slowly surrender its gold.

The Black Shoes

Now that you have come of age
I am going to give you my shoes.

You think them unfashionable,
you mourn their lack of heel.

But you can dance in these shoes,
change a tyre, unblock a drain.

More importantly you can dig a garden,
reap exactly what you sow.

The last twenty years I have had only these shoes,
the minute they die, they are reborn.

You can wear them with anything,
they will not pinch nor raise a blister.

They are good at funerals and christenings,
have attended at least one birth.

They were built to travel,
can circumnavigate the globe.

Their leather withstands rain, drought,
even tolerates the white crust of snow.

I give you these shoes because they are not so much shoes
but rather the way a seahorse propels itself through water.

Boats for the strong current,
they are tyres with thick, new tread.

These are the flinty iron of hooves, the solid wood
of clogs, they are shoes that do not know how to lie.

Their black is a year's supply of winter coal,
the jet beads on a dress at a dance during the Great War.

They are rationing, food stamps,
and a bread queue in Sarajevo's siege.

You can make your own bed and lie in it in these shoes,
you can have your cake and eat it.

I give you these flat, black shoes because sex
should not be worn upon the sleeve or the foot;

your culture says be aggressively vulnerable,
I say be vulnerably aggressive.

These shoes have no heel
so as to connect you to the earth,

the earth is in trouble,
I hear her voice through the soles of my feet;

she wants to ask why it is you came now,
what it is you have to offer?

Come child, in these shoes,
you need not be afraid to answer.

Dear Holdridge

Holdridge, I'm writing to tell you your toad is dead.
Remember the delight of giving that frog your name,
the pride you felt coming out of Carillo to find
those thousands of black and orange backs glinting like a river
in the Costa Rican sun? Who could have known
that such a day would come: searches of its last
remaining habitat have failed to turn up one.
Holdridge, I'm so sorry to tell you, your toad is gone.

Holdridge don't feel singled out, Bory's white bat,
Buhler's rat and Pemberton's mouse are perished too,
and Schomburgk's deer, that roamed the swampy plains
of Laos is only now a flitting ghost. Holdridge,
you're a man who surely understands the rational,
scientific mind—is it moved? Can you weep
for the Red River turtle, whose race, having survived
two hundred million years, is now reduced to just four beasts?

Holdridge would it grieve you to hear the Golden toad,
and the Harlequin, are also now extinct?
We've lost the Arabian ostrich and the Barbary lion,
Black rhino are vanished from Cameroon,
Bali and Tazmania have hunted down their final tigers,
Zanzibar its leopard, while in China the Yangtze river
flows a polluted, aquatic coffin, where fishing nets
have drowned the last Baiji dolphin.

Holdridge, I wonder could you offer us any small advice,
for they're saying the number of people on planet earth
is set to rise to nine billion in the next forty years,
they're sure the climate's changed, that topsoil's

being washed away at an alarming rate, and because
it takes a thousand litres of water to make two pints of milk,
our lakes and rivers are running dry. Holdridge,
tell me, how many more species will need to die?

Forgive the outburst, Holdridge, as I said,
I was only writing to tell you that your toad is dead,
a strangely purposeless amphibian, mute, deaf,
much of its life was lived with its head beneath the sand.
Likewise, that Baiji dolphin was ever an imperfect creature,
possessed of small eyes and reduced sight, it rested
in the slow current at night, and left us nothing but recordings
of the sound it made, a warning whistle,
                              audible beyond the watery grave.

Scissors

Boarding-pass and baggage, barefoot and shuffling,
I'm suddenly grateful for the way my unmoored eye
fixes on a Perspex box of nail-scissors.

An impossible puzzle of innumerable loops and minute blades.
A silver knot of redundant steel, incomprehensible but for
the occasional nail-file, the recognisable shield of a Swiss-army
    knife.

And I know I am not looking at many hundred failed hi-jacks,
but rather intimacies stolen from bathrooms and bedrooms,
moments of ordinariness tactile on the air. And I am put in mind

of the heaped spectacles, the gold watches and wedding bands
taken from Europe's Jews; how I have almost come to love
the Germans and their impossible history, the way it stands

like a mirror we must all look into once, as if it could reveal
how we might have fared, or would fare should it ever begin again—
I have few illusions, I might sleep it out in extravagant underwear,

in the arms of an officer, if someone asked I might take in a child.
But no grand heroics. Though we'd know, wouldn't we?
We'd recognise the earliest signs of persecution if we saw them.
                    We'd halt them in their tracks.

In Christchurch the Baker

for Libby Grant

When the first quake hit, his shop was destroyed—
only the oven was saved. He did what he could, baked
in the ruins, sold loaves from a van, navigating the broken streets,

the earth spewing up its wet gut, submerging his city
in *liquefaction*—this word no one had known but suddenly
needed to use daily to explain the wreckage of their lives.

The baker carried on, overlaying the new vocabulary onto the old,
until February's quake condemned even his ruined kitchen.
He salvaged what he could, built a bivouac in the back yard.

All winter he slept beneath canvas, fetched water from a spigot,
squatted over a privy. The streets emptied, those that stayed spoke
of insurance claims, default loans and mortgages on ruined homes.

The cathedral fell, churches were deconsecrated but slowly life
sprang through the cracks—someone set up a book swap
on the corner, kept its library in a fridge. The fates relented.

The baker found new premises, his thoughts returned to wheat
and barley and rye. He took a stall in the marketplace—
once again his days were cob, batch loaf, semmel.
                    Brioch, croissant, pretzel.
                            Pumpernickel, bannock, challah.

Becoming Animal

The Road of Excess Leads to the Palace of Wisdom

Let us say I was blown out to sea in a gale.

There is a tempest where chaos
happens all the time,

it isn't in the easy houses
along the shore.

I thought I was done with vortex
but I wasn't looking
and a wind swept me off my feet.

A small error of judgement
and you can lose years of your life.

But I'm back now. No surprise
that I should wash up on this island,

here is where the first impulse
for freedom began.

Two roads lead away from this cottage.

You can take the cliff path,
or go up over the mountains,

both lead to moments of grace.

Leaving

The sound of water gradually dims
to be replaced by the voice of the land:

sheep bleat from rocks,
a crow calls above the hill.

Soon someone laughs
and the talk returns

to erase all memory of how it was
to stand beneath the falls

and have their force
wash your life clean.

The mountains
release their grasp,

a civilised self was waiting for you
in the car park all along.

Glance back to where the stream
cuts a white cleft in the hillside—

you may glimpse your wildness
stepping down into the pool

and the pool itself dreaming of evening,
the spirit of place come
                              with cupped hands.

Equinox

Sometimes you have to be at the equinox
before the harvest comes in,

night equals day on every parallel,
you finally balance dark with light.

Mother-of-pearl sky stretches
above mother-of-pearl ocean,

and your children reap results, licences,
they cross the thresholds out of childhood.

You can't decide what scent to wear
as you move into the future,

and this man that you have always
forbidden yourself to look in the eye,

you may touch him now, he may touch you.

He Asks That She Explain Love

I. KILMALKALDEER

Three sycamores grow in the churchyard.
All spring, two huddle like spinster sisters,

their arms empty save the tight buds
they clasp against the sea wind.

The third, growing in the lee of the church,
dances in a shimmering, emerald green.

II. MAHON FALLS

Up there the elements exchange themselves,
spray turns to mist, mist turns to air,

air bubbles up within water,
water allows the soft rock to dissolve.

The peat-brown earth liquefies,
liquid takes on structure to form pools,

the pools mirror the sky.

The May Morning She Allows Herself to be Ophelia

It is the waterweed that invites me in,
offers a white bed and the river's constant touch.

Why not step down into water,
I have been drowning since you left.

Pale tendrils grow through my hair,
I wear a liquid crown.

Oh Hamlet, there were voices
that warned me against you,

but none saw you
would bring me down this far.

Let it be written on water that I loved you well—
prince beyond my star.

In the Aftermath

Mountains of grief. Then an Alpine depression
I crossed without faith. I dreamed of a sad woman
who lay down on her dog, and the dog carried her.
It was my dog-self that brought me through,

down into foothills where around each corner
I caught a glimpse of health only to have it elude me
again. Months it took. For this is what happens
when his wife leaves him and the man

you have always loved reaches out, only to
drop your open heart when it no longer suits his need.
In the aftermath I wanted to paint the word *Fraud*
on his practice door, but there was no way back

to that sacred place, and all I could offer my fury
was the cold with which I had said,
                    Don't ever touch another patient again.

On Waking

I gather myself from the four corners of my dreaming
but don't succeed, parts of me stay missing,

parts of me still leaving lovers I left years ago,
parts of me scrambling retreat from half-forgotten scenes.

Last night I burned my hand and cried out for help
unable to pull my fingers from the flames.

So long it takes to return from the dream roads
and only persuaded by a fragment of text I keep close,

Jung's garments burst into leaf.

Winter

I woke to a heron on what used to be my pond—
upright and regal in the mess of weed.

The once-clear surface of the pool
was an ugly green and what lived beneath it

was water heavy with clay, the lungs of that clay
so clogged with water they could not breathe.

The heron put its feet down into that morass
the way a tree will put roots into any ground,

and it stood waiting while I bathed and dressed—
forgetting about its presence—

only calling me back to the window, hours later,
to say it waited still. Not that it spoke, it was just

a heron patrolling the underbelly of the year
and finding what it needed and taking wing.

Winter is always thus. I wanted to think that bird
could draw from my stagnancy a fish

but the heron fed only on the scuttling creatures
the hooded crows live by

and I had to remember there are some things
that cannot be transformed

unless you bring them to Nature
and she is kind enough to prescribe

a dozen fieldfares clearing frosted grass,
a fox barking the limits of its territory

and claiming you as its own.

Pace

for Marianne Gabriel and Charlie Stephens

Like a woman who goes
to her lover's room when he is not there,
I go to the woods.

Like a woman laying her hand
on each of his possessions
and loving him all the more,

I walk in the trees and touch—
pine cone, leaf, feather, husk.
Always a longing to catch sight

of squirrel, badger, deer.
The forest pulling me deeper in
until the trees reveal

it's not a glimpse of wildness
that I crave, but more like
one of those stories

where the stranger welcomed
into the family home
turns out to be a fox,

or the fisherman's wife
after long years of marriage
proves to be a seal.

Sometimes my need is
to lie down beneath the pines,

to curl, heart to earth.
Only the breath. Only fur.

Requiem

Fur does not understand.
Fur licks its wounds. Fur curls.
All fur knows is threat.

Fur soothes itself over and over
but there is no soothing.

Once fur navigated the wild,
now fur navigates humanity.

The island of fur is growing smaller.
Fur has no words
in any of its languages for such loss.

Fur does not understand futility,
fur lives by hope.

Fur would like to communicate what needs to be said
but no place has been set for fur at the table.

Fur has long memory,
it was in the woods at Theresienstadt.

Fur is building a choir,
bring chairs for the executioners.

I Thought I Was Done with Those Poems

but then she took to wandering naked,
feeling wind and sunlight on her breasts.

Sometimes she squatted to relieve herself
beneath trees, beneath stars.

It became imperative
to do these things,

to know that she had been here,
creaturely, sensate on the earth.

Cornucopia

In God's Lemon Aspect

It was Anna who made this tile. Anna who painted the ceramic trees and set among their leaves three yellow baubles. Three drops of yellow glaze against a cerulean sky—lemons that my fingers trace like Braille. They are punctuation marks. They are globes. They are suns burnt out in a distant galaxy.

They resurrect the table at Jerpoint. All of us young, and someone is talking about temples, sanctuaries carved into mountains. Only the temples have fallen into disuse. They have become store-rooms: a place for the lemon harvest.

We quieten in the face of that disrepair, quieten until one of us says, *But imagine that—imagine a room full of lemons.*

Lemon stacked on lemon. Lemon shape. Lemon skin. Yellow on yellow on yellow. The air citrus, dazzling, making sunlight of a sort. The acid juice untasted. And the room a temple still.

For so many years I have carried these store-rooms with me. But it was Anna who knew to fix the lemons to this tile. I love the way they feel beneath my fingers, love the harvest they gather in.

The Egg Collection

I should not love them for these are the birds
that grew cold and never were allowed to live—
but what shimmers around these eggs
is not death but living wing,
as though they hold not just their own young
but all the generations
since my boy-father first collected them.

The smallest is no larger than my smallest nail,
the seeds of pumpkins are not so small,
yet furled birds break loose
from just such eggs year after year.
Only now I read some latest human caper
is souring the soil, destroying snails,
and the birds are laying unviable eggs.

It is harder to live having heard such news—
but it makes me love the collection all the more.
Against such harm I've placed a papier-mâché wren
above the eggs where they hang in my hall.
And though I know wren and eggs will never fly—
I feel they do. Each time I pass them they gift me
the spirit of flight, the presence of bird after bird.

When the Animals Leave They Take Their Medicine With Them

The last Irish wolf was eradicated in 1786.
In 1950 Britain had thirty-six million hedgehogs,
in 2013, one million.

And Otter, putting down her rudder,
ceased to steer.

Heron abandoned slow grace.
Owl forsook wisdom.

Flocks of field-birds refused to rise as one.
Stag ceased to guard the herd.

Fox extinguished her coat's red flame.
Squirrel left off prudent reserve.

In their pool the speckled trout
gave up camouflage.

Moth stopped searching
for the light.

Badger released his jaw
and let go the fragile earth.

But then some mystery

and otter began again to steer.
Heron resumed slow grace.

Owl reclaimed foresight.
Lark lifted her song above the moor.

Again the bees
passed on the steps of their dance.

Again caterpillar entered the chrysalis
and took on the arduous task of transformation.

Again badger set a tenacious jaw.

Two Walks at Lavigny

i

In soft rain we walked around the stubble field
and you talked about giving-up alcohol,
how raw you were, slippery and vulnerable
as a newborn child, and you were new born
to yourself, wailing insecurity. And I knew
what it was like to be in your too-thin body,
to be lost in yourself, and the way from that maze
was a thread that would need to be spun
word by impossible word.

I loved you then in the soft rain of the empty field
because there I was speaking from your mouth,
breathing from your hesitant lungs,
spilled unready into an astonishing world.

ii

It was Kaiser who invited me into the evening,
Kaiser who led the way to the valley, green
like a faience bowl decorated with vines
and a river running through it, the sides
of the bowl so steep we curved a way down into
the dusk, the two of us talking about Solidarity
and when The Wall came down, making our way
to the vine-keeper's hut where we sat until
all light had leeched from the evening,
Kaiser talking of South Africa, how he'd been
with the mothers of sons tortured to death
And those women, they were not bitter. So there
like gold flecks in the glaze of the valley's bowl
were their stories and the gilt river of Kaiser
quoting Mandela, *Revenge is not an option.*

It was a hidden valley and we went into it together
but who can say at what point the valley came into us.
How porous will you let yourself be to this life?
I want that valley to seep into my bedrock.
I want to take it with me to the end of my days,
when I pass over, it will fly back out of me
the way they once believed bees flew
from bugonia bulls. How permeable
will you be to this life? I want everything
to course with the blood through my veins.

A Cure for November

First gather coloured silks. Find those that bear
the names of flowers, violet, lilac, lavender;
take the hues of precious stones, turquoise, amber, jade.

Find tangerine, apricot, a dazzling lime.
Work in eggshell blue. Put the red from a robin's breast
beside gold so it lights like a fire in the hearth.

Take from the shelves a dictionary of stitches,
re-learn the old tailoring, use God's eye stitch,
French knots, a plain herringbone.

Look about your house for loose objects,
beads, ribbon, a twist of string,
pin them to the folds of this cloth.

Choose a thread and let it sew out
the contents of your mind, each stitch
a metaphor for a relationship, or a regret.

Trust when the needle plunges
beneath fabric to move unseen
the way laylines run below Avebury Henge.

Take cobalt blue and let your steady breath
illuminate, just as stained glass lights
on Remembrance Sunday when a lone bugler

plays 'The Last Post' in notes poppy red.
Add rain on the window, the way it falls
without fear or longing. Accept the accident

when you prick your finger and suddenly
there is a living drop of blood that you wipe
in the mouth the way women have done forever.

Take silver thread and wool soft as summer cloud,
place them in dialogue, let them speak out all
you have not found the strength to say.

Put in embarrassment, peppermint green envy,
and jaundiced yellow for your dull days;
darn them here beside your worst faults.

Unpick regret. In India it is the Festival of Light:
they are setting small candles onto the holy river.
Cease your despair, employ a deep, personal witchcraft,

sew your life back together, stitch by stitch.

I Packed My Bag

and in it I put the things specified on their list:
dressing-gown and slippers, toothbrush and paste.
I squashed in a decent pillow and my favourite books.
I snuck in a box of chocolates.

I added the opening bars of Bach's cello suite in G,
and the Vee Valley when the rhododendrons bloom.
I put in salt spray crashing off Hook Head,
and silence from the top of Sliabh na mBan.

There would be hours of waiting
and sometimes they would take my dignity,
so I put in endurance, and a smile for a stranger,
and an acre of meadow in soft rain.

Lastly, I packed water bottled at Brigit's Well,
and an old piece of paper
on which I'd copied down: 'Our single purpose
is to magnify the light we share between us.'

All Year

All year I told myself *Listen,*
that sound in the wind, that's God.

And when the soft rain fell, I said
There's God falling in the meadows.

I praised the snowdrops, the daffodils
and the tulips when they came.

The swallows returned as if
those in exile had come home.

But all year I got things wrong,
I made mistakes that hurt people,

I was confused by the state of the world
and the actions of others,

I complained often and sometimes bitterly.
I don't believe I saved anyone's life.

But I kept on listening
for the sound of God in the wind,

kept on watching the soft rain
bring God to the meadows,

and every morning I read the same
small note to myself. *Faith*, it said. *Courage.*

Balance

for Sinéad Morrissey

The parting in my hair falls to the left
like a train track or an iron curtain
dividing a continent.

In my crane bag I carry a bikini-clad lady
who once stood in front of a target
while a man threw knives.

In my crane bag I carry the lattice
of a skeletal leaf, and a bronze
war-memorial angel.

In my crane bag I carry
the gossamer of bat wing,
and the red brick that built Belfast.

Homes have foundations, trees
put down roots, but something stops
my left foot from touching the ground.

The ship pitches. I stumble from stern
to prow. The figurehead is a Madonna,
Stella Maris, Our Lady of the Seas;

navigating ocean, bare-breasting storm.

Pomegranate

for Lani O'Hanlon

September was the first, late sun,
sudden loss.

October brought a language of decay,
mushrooms, lichen, liver-spots on her skin.

She swallowed, and birthed November—
grey month of continuous rain.

And sucking the next seed, she sucked light
from the sky, let night conquer December.

Not a winged insect alive on the air,
she created a January so raw it engendered courage.

She put another in her mouth
and set free the sharp frosts of February—

how bittersweet the pips, their ruby flesh
so sensuous, the white seed tart and bitter.

She smiled and winced,
tears in her eyes,

eyes watering in the March wind,
her lips stained with sugar.

Light

for Mark

Early winter, and you are heating soup in the kitchen
months only since your fall in the mountains,

and, with your neck twice-broken, you are slow
but own a calm I'm jealous of.

In the sun-room, I look out into your garden,
which is a way of looking into your heart;
pink late lilies bloom there and white cyclamen.

Sunlight floods your heron meadow,
sunlight curls in the last leaves on the wisteria,

and finds chink enough to enter this room
with its vase of flowers,
turning their stems translucent green,

so I am suddenly graced to see
that light is only made complete
by what it touches.

In the dim kitchen you make your progress,
neither of us ready yet to speak
of this imperishable urge of light

to know itself by what it falls upon.

Evening Star

I dreamed of whales, huge whales
coming into a bay, coming close.

Weeks after, seals lifted themselves out of the ocean
to climb the rocks beneath my window.

Then a rhino appeared. An angry elephant
pushed at the car I was driving.

That summer I read the Holy Spirit appears to us
in dreams. I had expected something that looked like God.

But then a river flowed red with copper,
and the earth and stones around it were russet too.

The alchemists say copper represents
Venus, planet and Goddess both.

Tell me, how does Spirit move in your dreams?

Happiness Writes White

for my brother, Henry Wells

"Le Bonheur ecrit a l'encre blanche sur des pages blanches"
—*Henry Millon de Montherlant*

If happiness writes in white ink on a white page
then it also writes in white hawthorn across the May hills,

taking its taper to elder, to ignite the creamy-white,
pollen-heavy heads of happiness.

If happiness writes in white ink on a white page
it also writes in ermine, in Arctic fox

and on the wet backs of Beluga whales. Happiness
spirals its white into the mother-of-pearl of sea shells,

ices itself into the milk-white of frozen lakes,
announces itself in swans' wings on the white air.

For so long happiness was unfamiliar,
then it placed its white wafer on my tongue.

Go on, it said, let me write in the weave
of white linen hung on your line to dry.

And when happiness asked to be habitual,
I bought it seven white shirts.

If I am wearing white it means I am happy,
I have found a way to live in the world.

River

for Margaret Organ

What you loved was the mirror of the river,
how the purple mountain turned liquid and flowed downstream.

What you loved was the alder releasing mauve catkins,
and the women setting white boats onto the tide.

You loved squatting down in the mud and wet roots,
watching the wings of small flocks fly overhead.

The river belonged to the birds. The only violence was the arrow
of a cormorant, the only anger was the heron's piercing cry.

What you loved was seeing Her in the water, the Cailleach
in Her cloak, and on the riverbank, the artist in her mantle.

Myth

Like leaves the old ambitions
fell away.

Instead snail shells
bleached white by time

and twigs hung
with beach-casing stars.

She wove a nest from
branches spalted with decay.

Her eyes traced the limbs of trees
and everywhere saw sculpture.

Like leaves the old expectations
fell away,

unhelpful aspirations spun down
with seeds of sycamore.

Instead the sane harvest
of beech mast,

the modest currency
of acorn.

In the hazel trees
she was kernel,

and, when she fell, it was only deeper
into the salmon pool.

Aegis

Offering is given at the end in thanks, and the maze that led
to the antique shop in Venice's ghetto was a pilgrimage of
        twenty years.

Two rough decades—if there wasn't drama, there was crisis,
perpetual worry, a surfeit of strife. But not alone for love

is the heart made, and you children gave me courage—
a near invisible presence more like absence

until I saw it manifest in the antique-shop window, pinned
among small metal limbs—the aegis of two silver breasts.

All through your childhood I had leaned into their curve.
Now that you are leaving home, there comes a natural tally—

so many things I failed to provide, but the ex-voto breastplate
upholds, reassures me there was always milk.

Ex-voto

for Sliabh and Holly

Jasmine budding into flower, oranges
ripening, we had our first foreign holiday.

It was all beginnings and endings,
last responsibilities, new freedom.

Olivia so drunk she fell
off the curb into traffic.

Holly's neck purpled with love-bites
from a Cuban boy she met on a bus.

I was so surrounded by teenagers
I became one of them,

thinking of little more than mojitos,
ice and mint and sugar.

Mornings I was alone, in palaces and galleries,
and the archaeological museum

where I fell in love
with a wall of votive offerings,

Roman footprints carved in stone
and the simple lettering: ex voto.

Ex voto, my darlings,
for the journey and return.

NOTES

'Autumn', p.27
The phrase "rough, dumb country stuff" belongs to Sylvia Plath. It comes from some of my favourite lines in her poem 'By Candlelight'.

'Pyx', p. 46
Pyx is a late Middle English word for box. In the Christian church, consecrated bread is kept within the pyx. This poem was created in response to artworks by Bernie Leahy, in particular her 'Hope Artefact' series, a set of boxes that held plaster replicas of a child's hand, in the manner of holy relics.

'In Christchurch the Baker', p.62
Since 4.9.2010 Christchurch, New Zealand, has experienced more than 10,000 earthquakes. This poem was inspired by the baker featured in Gerard Smyth's documentary 'When a City Falls'.

'The Road of Excess Leads to the Palace of Wisdom', p.65
The title of this poem is one of William Blake's 'Proverbs of Hell'.

'When the Animals Leave They Take Their Medicine With Them', p.83
"When the animals leave they take their medicine with them", was a phrase used by the late, and much-missed, Irish philosopher John Moriarty.

'Becoming Animal', p.63
The title of this section of poems pays tribute to the sane and profound writings of cultural ecologist David Abram. I am particularly grateful for his influential book *Becoming Animal: An Earthly Cosmology.*

'Requiem', p.76
Theresienstadt makes reference to the garrison city of Terezín, now in the Czech Republic, which was used by the Nazis as a

concentration camp during the Second World War. Many artists, writers and musicians were imprisoned there and Nazi propaganda publicized the camp for its rich cultural life. Piano recitals, concerts and choral pieces were performed for the benefit of the regime. Most famously, Verdi's 'Requiem'.

'Balance', p.91
The Crane bag is a potent totem from Irish myth. The bag was originally created by Mannanán Mac Lir from the skin of a crane, the magically transformed body of his deceased lover, Aoife. The crane bag was bottomless, it carried every precious thing Mannanán Mac Lir owned. It also contained language, hounds and birds. Further reference is made to the Crane Bag in 'Bosnia 2015' p.44, and is explored differently in 'Pyx' p.46. Other allusions to this idea are scattered throughout the collection, which is in itself something of a meditation on what each of us carries beneath the skin, beneath the fur.

Lightning Source UK Ltd.
Milton Keynes UK
UKHW010656210422
401838UK00005B/193